The Point of
Ripeness

a collection of poems

The Point of Ripeness

Ripeness

a collection of poems

Peter Makem

Appletree Press

This work is dedicated to my wife Catherine
and children Gráinne and Colm.

First published in 2002 by
Appletree Press Ltd
The Old Potato Station
14 Howard Street South
Belfast
BT7 1AP

A catalogue record for this book is available from
the British Library.

The Point of Ripeness – A Collection of Poems

ISBN 0-86281-845-1

10 9 8 7 6 5 4 3 2 1

The publisher and writer gratefully acknowledge
the patronage of Gerard and Margaret O'Hare,
Rostrevor, which made the publication possible.

CONTENTS

Celtic Tiger

We have turned with rancour
On our fathers,
We have spat out all
That tasted of their way,
Taking the comely maiden's hand
Who smiled and called our name,
And now, trimmed with fortune,
Now stood on dark pages
Speak the Elysian Fields,
Speak long of bloom and blossom.
Still and all, as jig and reel
Race to take our step
The old gods, motionless,
Watch us eye their script,
Watch us slowly scan the plot –
"Be blessed, now and ever more.
The point of ripeness
Is the point of rot."

But We Were Drunk Then

Cromwell fresh from Wexford town
And the dark set of blood.
Cromwell's reassembled throng,
Brattle of armour, strike of shod
Return to the camp, line by line
For prayers of thanksgiving,
For hymn and victory song,
And into sleep, and night's toss – *Oh then?*
But we were drunk then.
Somebody set us drunk.
Someone slipped drink into our glass.

Only should blinding light come
Would Pizzaro lament the Inca dead,
Or Titus mourn Jerusalem,
Or Herod grip his head in shame.
Only should light strike
Would Paul of Tarsus beg the dark
In skin locked at eyelid
And moan, and curse – *Oh then?*
But we were drunk then.
Somebody set us drunk.
Someone slipped drink into our glass.

Our piper's fingers shaped the ancient
Impulse of the race, a first cry
From first born, the story went,
Departing from a lover's balm
Moved off half soul, half body,
Tossed, twisting storm as calm
And every motion the possession
Of the vanished lover.
Our singers sang around that tune.
Dancers stepped it up the floor.

And dusk is full of beginnings,
High above the fulcrum
Beyond the starling and the plover
Glowing warrior and lover
Soar upon the shores of day
Until their wings fall away.
Only at the still pendulum
Might lips move, whisper pass – *Oh then?*
But we were drunk then.
Somebody set us drunk.
Someone slipped drink into our glass.

They live on Paradise, they
Moving under long oppression
Bring their flower in full blossom
Before the arc of dawn.
Rendered old, rendered young with pain
Stand attention to their dream,
And all that is not of Eden
Hated in the oppressor's way,
All who should feed the root
Of the forbidden fruit,

And war it is. War the call.
The tidal surge won't turn
Until its moon is spent.
Prayers floats there, supplication
On the shore bound swell
And rock and great rock shaken.
After, the seas, the shrunken, penitent
Seas far out lap remorse – *Oh then?*
But we were drunk then.
Somebody set us drunk.
Someone slipped drink into our glass.

Let Tone and Emmett
Rest in Peace

Let Tone and Emmett rest in peace.
The throbbing centuries be done.
The wind is down, daybreak is close,
The night is filling up with dawn.

Behind their tombs from a grey rim
At contours loosening the dark
Clearing heads take shape, features come
In the slow morning sculptor's work,

And slow figures move out
With scroll and habit clearing there,
And walk toward the milky light,
And vanish with the morning star.

I thought that on arriving, and day
Drying the dew's embrace I heard
From close to where they lay
A quiet chanting word by word –

Let us dare to drop our wounds,
Let us dare to walk unaided,
Moving unto hallowed grounds
Untrodden since the age of Clonard –

For Tone and Emmett, Pearse and all
Who soldiered out their brotherhood
Were bonded by the ancient's quill,
By orpiment and kermes' bleed

That surging turmoil of the dusk,
The lapis sky, the purple verge
Of folium, yolk spill, face and mask
Writhing, twisting on their page.

They knew those times, knew Gall
And Fiacre, knew well Killian and Fergal,
Columbanus, Colmcille,
And meditate their deepest call,

And meditate their deepest dream
That we be free to rise the pen,
And raise our banner in their name,
And we be glorious again.

And that day be with us now and be
As then, the glowing mind of the world,
No limb nor stream, no extremity –
We poured our melt into their mould,

Melt beyond those times, melt that drove
Our fathers into the midwinter glare,
And all that trapped beginning still alive
In veins and bones, now, like spring water

Seeps its fresh life, bends the diviner's rod,
And we, untouched by the clot of thought
That dried up Greek and Roman head
Hear youthful voices calling out

To walk among them once again.
We hear this. These voices, near, far
Who need our sunset for their dawn,
We of Clonmacnoise and Bangor,

We of our daytime know their night
To soar on those tumultuous pages
And once again the fire to light
This second coming of the dark ages.

Then Tone and Emmett rest in peace.
And Ireland guard the sacred earth.
And move toward their resting place
With quiet step, with quiet breath,

And then in prayer and blessing done
Before we turn to take our leave,
Pluck the flowers that have grown,
And place them gently on their grave.

Causeway

Beyond the restless edges
Of the tectonic plates
Antrim's form is cast and set.
Beyond the fracture lines
That woke up Alp and Himalaya,
The third, the final lava spill
Fulfilled all assertions.
At a placc east of Dunluce
Its slowing motion darkened
Into the black clot,
Year on year after year
Cooling in the sun's heat,
Warm in the cool of the moon.
And there, out from the solid depth
Faint sound as chanting rose,
Rising pitch, racing scale
Broke out to its sky
In a final convulsion.
They face toward the ocean
Like seals crowded on a shore,
The face to the horizon
In their hexagonal wait
Century by century
At tidal wash and parting,
Antrim's forms one by one
Step back to the clot of dark,
Step forward into dawn.

The Hunger

1

At the parting of Forty Seven
In the great shedding of skin
We moved still wet
Out of our cracked scale.
We had known this of old and thought
The tide of things re grow
Its flesh and all scar and heal,
Watched it now crack again
Layer after layer until
By Forty Nine the bare bone,
Bone dry of marrow
Ended our expectation.

2

We had thought until then
That they who lorded over us
Must have mercy on us.
We had thought the great plight
Might bring the great repeal
And name our names, raise us, raise us,
Christ, we prayed night to night,
We prayed to dream and child's call
And call again, and dream again,
Into gull and gannet wail,
Into voices telling us
Nature itself was evicting us.

3

Out on the Atlantic shoreline
The tidal lungs of ocean move.
Beyond drought, beyond rain,
Beyond the river's offering
Flow and hollow fill and leave.
We stay awhile, we stand and hear
The turn at dawn, the morning roar
Into evening's long lament
Face past our moment,
Sound past our lingering.
And now must ride the ghostly boat
And enter blindly to it's keep,
Enter down the ocean's plight
The lunar craving of the deep.

4

Slow movers in the Sinai
Forge their sandy waves.
Behind, the Red Sea line
As a glow of distant land
Holds out on the horizon.
They stop. They turn. They face west
The great concourse,
A minute's silence to their saviour
Thinning between heaven and earth.
The dusk settles to their quiet.
The moments hold the vast peace
Until a shout breaks it up
And all turn and move again,
The city on the march
In full deliverance,
On toward the kingdom,
To the milk, to the wild honey,
Old heads full of freedom.
Young heads full of victory.

Too Bright, Too Soon Your
Star Appeared

Too bright, too soon, your star appeared,
Too west the fanning wind,
And though you lie an ember now
Below your slow burning peer,
Leave them be, let them burn,
Your white ash is come of fire
Older winds will fan and flare,
Older winds will touch and enter,
Old, old, the ancient wind.

Maybe at a sunset you have stood
Trembling as the trembling sun
Like an old age eye at sleep's call
Sink beneath a closing lid,
And face toward the lost dawn,
And bitter thoughts glow and brighten,
And face toward the west again
In the last shreds of heaven's fall.

Maybe only an aged hermit
In a wild sea-broken place
Wail his vast untroubled peace.
Maybe he, for whom no god or prophet
Broke a promise breath the air
As deep as youth, day long or star,
And endless raise of arm to bless
The endless race of wilderness.

Maybe the ages knew it in their bones.
The ages made it into song,
They tormented by their dawns
Still and all followed dark,
And somewhere into sleep
Entered the flow of dreaming
All the sunlit night, and a breath drop,
And rise, and voice strain to speak,

Voice after long inhale, a gravel rattle
In the sea's departing swell
And the return of breath
At shoreline froth
From skins of air
As one who never spoke before,
Sounding out of the suds
The slow, full deliberate words –

Do not enter. Do not enter
Fresh from March to bloom
Into the summer's core.
Do not feed that sweetest dream
You alighting from your loft,
Do not spread that wing to ride,
A wing no wind will lift,
An air no gull can glide –

Maybe the absence is the creation –
In the parting is the coming, and until
We bear what can not be borne,
Unless we raise what can not be lifted,
Until no one hears our last call,
Until no one knows our route or road
The waters will not divide,
The Red Sea remains in flood.

Too bright, too soon your star appeared,
Too west the fanning wind,
And though you lie an ember now
Below your slow burning peer,
Leave them be, let them burn,
Your white ash is come of fire
Older winds will fan and flare,
Older winds will touch and enter.
Old, old, the ancient wind.

The Jotter

I returned to some old verse
In the middle pages of a jotter
About a lover and his lass
I had written there years before,

And after staring for a time
Ringed words to make a change,
Soften rhythm, soften rhyme,
Pluck, stitch, re-arrange.

I read aloud and re-read
The lines of my amendment,
But old words reared their head,
And jarred there, and broke my chant,

And noun recoiled and drew in
Its adjectives around it
As verb and preposition
Soured to my edit.

And when I went to read again
I found a fractured couplet,
And fresh lines broken down,
And fresh words thrown about.

I pulled and probed their clinging
To part one from the other,
The more I forced the editing,
The tighter clung together.

I stopped. I erased my pencil scars,
Set the jotter in its place
And left them there, old lovers,
In their newly locked embrace.

I Will Walk These Rims

I will walk these rims of Ulster
For now and forever more,
At late and early twilight time
Along the heavens' ocean,
And when her tidal rise is come,
Will journey on, will step afoot
Into the water of sunset,

Into the milk of dawn.

Titanic

From the centre
Of the polar Galaxy,
Her body forms.
Out of the spiral rims,
The immaculate, unbriny stars,
The slow, turning, winding layers
Raises up her arms.
Soon a descending figure
Will touch the Arctic crown,
In the long twilight shimmer there
Stand under dusk and dawn.

Before the forming came,
Before she took that form
Had fled without child
Into the night's cloudy fold
And racing moon and bay.
They cast her out, they mocked her roar
At every rivet and hammer struck
As the great shape, belly and back,
Along the gantry, plate by girder,
Raised its triumphant body.

New she turns her head
Toward the watery void,
And on her solemn face,
And on her flowing mantle
A glow as the Aurora Borealis.
It is neither day light nor moon light.
It is neither dusk light nor dawn light,
And she, abiding her oath,
Remains motionless until
At the chosen hour
Steps from her place
Into the mist of Labrador,
And moves south.

If There Be No Resurrection

If there be no resurrection
In vain do the builders build.

If after flash and tremor,
If after shake and thunder
Clouding shimmer not appear
That out from there, swell on swell
Vague forms hardening,
Returning forms step clear
To write down the unwritten,
To sing the great unsung,
In vain has Ireland measured stone,
Vain the dawn been held,
In vain the stylus, vain the scroll,
In vain do the builders build.

If we make return to the land
Blessing God for his peace
And settle down nine to five
Humming the odd verse
Of this and that forgotten love,
Fill a measure, raise a glass
To the newest fad and trend,
All, all and all is vain,
Chanter, bellows, bag and drone,
And vain have the tears meandered,
In vain the waves of guilt,
Vainly call and cry ascended
After dead and the dead lowered,
In vain have the builders built.

If Ulster's sons and daughters
Enter not the salmon turn
And move up freshening waters
Fresh parr ventured down,
Not arrive from where they swam,
Not appear at empty tomb
The grief will surely fall, the great glow
Surely darken, the people murmur, sigh
For blessed days under pharaoh
That one rise up, inhale and cry –
"Where now the promised land?
Where is the blood our lamb spilt?
Where is roof and rafter's bond
With the house that the builders built?"

If the world does not sense us,
If the world do not rise an ear
And fin vibrato, wing strum,
Clamour up upon our shore
To whisper pointing out toward us,
Whisper under brightening eyes –
These are the ones, settle here,
These are of oldest wisdom,
These are the new wise –
In vain and vain the ages' stir,
Whatever named, whatever willed,
In vain the ice, in vain the fire,
In vain are all the centuries.
In vain did the builders build.

Sellafield

We scanned those seas for Viking
In the dawn sun, for Norman boat

Stared into fog, our ears sprung
At tidal whisper, our heart beat

Loud in the still night. These waters
That took the crystal ice-age roof

Had long before under moon and stars
Danced around the birth of life,

And all the million years' plan
That shoals teem rich seas

Now find the plot undone
Reversing vast complexities,

The rhyme of oar we cannot hear,
The sails unseen and speeding prow

And we, still into our prayer
Of thanks, watching new things grow,

Things bud, bloom out of long dreams,
Have not reached "amen" before

The beads fall, old faces and names
Enter with the dreaming's stir,

Old dreadings, old despair
In the tide and the wind and rain,

Turning us to the conqueror,
Strongbow, Cromwell come again.

In Paradiso

Under the world's skin,
Beneath the eyes of land and ocean
Unheeded rages pace.
Only at Etna's shout, or Krafla,
Or the shaking of the door
At Agadir and San Andreas
Do heads rouse and turn before
Lapsing at lull and cooling lava.

Once they were pitied, these
Named as Death and Death,
And when their muffled voices
Clamoured stars, their breath,
Froth, shaping the world's balm,
Yes, to call and roar pity came,
They sinking under their skin
Land, sea and all that dwell therin.

But we are settled now and old
We of the sea and the land,
Our set hearts can not endure
What throbs on below our world,
And curse this of human kind,
Curse that this might disappear,
We, moving on the pedestal
Of their burning, writhing spiral.

Night after night the holy one,
The demon come, and one wild face
As Cromm Cruagh, as Gargoyle,
Joyous feature and grimace
On the wide swinging thorible.
The daylight will slow all down,
A fleeting stare come
On the face of the blank pendulum.

Now, deeper in their sunken place
Roars die and die. The tremor
Of their passage as a great throat
Swallowing shakes once and no more.
The fire, the fire has taken them
They who came from fire.
The fire has not forsaken them
They whose love was fire.

At the heart of the great furnace
Brightness as solar fusion
A shade of body, a flawless face
Lies motionless. The noon or dawn
There opens its glassy eyes,
And raising itself from an elbow
Into its fullest rise
Moves around in the inferno.

That You Be Named
Among The Names

*Dedicated to all those who worked to create
the Peace, Good Friday 1998*

That you be named among the names,
That you be named to stand with those
Who stood the tremor of their times,
I call upon the heart's repose,
I call down the deepest dreams
And speak that you be numbered there
Who gave the leaven to our rise,
Who gave the rhyming to our rhymes,
And you be there, and you be there
Where dream and day roll their drums,
And you be stood the heart's applause.
And you be named among the names.

These need no pedestal.
Nor sculptor carve a title.
They need no monument or hall -
Too deep for that - too deep
For common ways, the people
Know them in their sacrifice,
The people raise them up
In bloom time and baring time,
In thorn time and time of rose
Rising voices form their name.

Then let us speak, and let us say,
And say though human veins espoused
The normal rite of natures way,
The doubt, the dread, the flesh and blood –
Say all this and say again –
That heart still opened up our dawn,
That heart still filled the empty west,
And you forever light our road,
And you be blest, and you be blest,
Flame of the morning, evening flames.
And you be named where hearts are raised.
And you be named among the names.

Acupuncture

I think of a white haired figure
Bent over Ireland
With their acupuncture needles
In the hood of the left hand.
Woman or man under
The shawl of fallen locks
I watch slow bony fingers
Insert into a drumlin col
Between Armagh and Monaghan,
And raising a head and lowering
Breathing coming as a sleeping child,
Implant, slowly, deeply
Into joints of rock and bog. Then
In the tongue of the Bann
Entering Lough Neagh
Pierce firmly throatward,
Needles set along the Boyne,
A needle entered in Kinsale
And one deep at Ferrycarrig.
Again I watch the bony fingers aim
Poised above Slieve Gullion
Between the Ring and mountain,
Between the mountain and the Ring,
And all day slaved away,
All night under the moon
To the dawn hour's entry,
Oak came and broom and hazel,
Ash and sycamore and elm

Sprouting at the filling east,
Filling hollow, crowding hill,
And away at an eye's meander,
Away at the distant river side
A rough sailing boat
Smaller and smaller there
Departing on the Foyle tide.

Sometimes

Sometimes I long to be
In some pre-Cambrian valley
Under the moon's early face,
Somewhere there look down
And watch her shadow trace
Along the eager dust and stone,
She riding the strange sky
Of forming plough and galaxy.

Somewhere there, somewhere then
In the barren moonlit valley
Hear fiddlers and piping men,
Hear their reel and slow air
Thin as the tone of a played saw,
This one's cran, that one's slur,
All the familiar styles
Along the moon filled miles.

So much youth was there.
The unblemished countenance,
Her molten glow in the noon
Of dark and lightest dance
Along the points of heaven.
And as I stare into her stare
I think toward the moving west,
And things moving in the east,

And I think again, in that place
Of no tomb or print of motion,
No sign of root nor bone
That some well featured race
Moves around when dawn light
Darkens risings of the night.
And I break into a prayer.
And I long to be there.

Sometimes I long to be
Among the long departed.
Sometimes, so close, so far,
Draw fallen eye and head
Toward the milky galaxy,
To the plough and the pole star.
And pipe and fiddle rise again.
And dancers in the rising moon.

Villanelle
I will set fire to the eternal hills

I will set fire to the eternal hills,
I will strike shadows where men dread the dark,
And childs' cries will linger, and old age calls

When I pronounce on early jigs and reels.
And I will light up hollows where men lurk,
I will set fire to the eternal hills.

And I will white the crows and black the gulls
And hang a red breast on the rising lark,
And childs' cries will linger, and old age calls,

And even if clouds mount the blazing swells
And voices plead with rains to drown my spark,
I will set fire to the eternal hills

That when glowing faces brown, burn to skulls,
Drooped heads light up, bright cracks fissure and fork,
And childs' cries will linger, and old age calls.

I will set fire to the eternal hills.
I will strike shadows where men dread the dark.
And childs' cries will linger and old age calls.
I will set fire to the eternal hills.

The Musicians

I knew them in their arriving
Night after night, and felt the stall
Of feet, the slow door creaking
At the entrance to their ritual.
Many a time I arose a while
To sit with them in their circle,

And watched the fingers fall and rise
In unison. No drum
Marked time nor bodhran beat
Broke the lock on their eyes,
The bow arm pendulum,
And the heart pound of their feet.

But I was young then. Maybe seven.
Maybe undisturbed by thought then
That the chanter lilt or moan
In freed and covered mouths carried me,
The oxter lungs, the drone on drone
Woman and man of the boortree.

Years after I knew I heard
That race of sound again, the cran
And shake, triplet and turn
In gathering of migrating bird,
Confused with certainty, wheel and cry
Their wild fling in the sky.

But they were gone, the music men
When I awoke to search from them,
The fiddler gone, the piper gone,
And cold gathered to the ashes,
And cold gathered around their chairs
When I awoke to search for them.

Along the headrig of a ploughed acre
Facing north in the north wind
I trail the skies to evening's shore
Until the darkness sets me blind.
And dawn and day, by day, by dawning,
Watch, will wait on their returning.

TEN SONNETS

1.Second Coming

Cold winds from the north grew wilder, puckered
The face and flared hair. Loaded bush and tree
Flew comet tail and bent. Long before, we
Had heard the call of animal and bird.
It is the ice again. The ice. It's her
Again. Something has stirred the white anger,
Some unbalancing aroused the passion,
Swollen, risen out on the horizon.
It is the conqueror again. She tramps
To war again. The march is on, taking
All in her stride, growth and rising, old ramps
And barriers of former battle, ring
And granite rampart, then, piles up and slumps
To silence. That was her second coming.

2. The Thaw

For an age she stayed and all was at rest.
For an age the fallen heavens covered her,
The young and the old lands, the spoils of war
Taken down, taken into her conquest.
Then one dusk grinding noise and colour came.
Then one dawn the east parted, full of flame
And the deep sound deepened and went again
Returning with a powerful contraction.
A dark shape, just beneath, rising, a form,
A grey skull, a pointed head breaking free
From the rims of tension, and closer come,
Water dripping, water running, we see
The breaking ice, the heave and push and ram
Of the mother and her half born baby.

3. Newcomers

Head by head they come the drumlin brood, wet
And smooth, crowning out into their full girth
Head by head as great sores where they break out,
Shedding mother skin in birth after birth.
It is a naked place, echo empty.
Now the rains feed ready for the mouth. The sun
Dries off the dripping and warms the body
As the young take in the air. Maybe one
Will face westward, eastward, and their heads, full
Or gaunt and fixed forever in the cast
The sculptor dealt them, must live eternal
Separation. They mark shapes from the mist.
Shadows tap them. They know slopes in the stream.
They called out their names before we named them.

4. Stone Age

All has settled down now. The hills are plush
And grown rich in their deciduous flows.
The ash and beech, the larch and the wild rush
Merge season easily. Snow kisses and goes.
But stone that locked and stone that broke away
Snared our father's wander, they, faced to east
In cut and fit toward the arc of day
Awoke from measuring, stood up to rest.
And in the bloom of nightfall under star
And meteor and under moon, rhythm
Took their breath, song took to song, hour on hour
Until the twilight came and covered them.
And day surprised the night with measured work.
And night lit up the places day made dark.

5. The Messenger

By the hedges stitched with twine and broom root
I stood beneath a cloud of March and thought
Of dead forms under the great ice, of war
And conquest, here, on this blessed acre.
I thought of the messenger wind, the rains'
Caress and mist embrace on the drumlin,
I thought of this among the grey, bare whins,
Growth as tiny bones swell and stretch and green,
But she will not return. Now, years after,
I know her body worn out in death's wear
Is fading limb by limb and soon all bones
Past ash and dust vanish in the earth's veins.
I thought of the messenger wind and swear
No song would come to make lament for her.

6. Things Done

I have no written evidence that I
Had fathers before my great grandfather,
All my lineage represented by
An entry in the parish register.
Beyond this, I watch on a woman bent
Across her stick, and at her side a man
Buckled down, both staring outward, both gaunt
Fix their eyes on me and then slowly turn.
Things done leave things undone as paths taken
Leave a trail. I thought one long trembling hour
Their footprints stretched away into Eden,
A dawn before had stood resplendent there.
But they were gone and never spoke my name.
Nor path, nor trail, not shaping of a dream.

7. Macha

I thought of a great shape on Macha's Fort
Whose eyelids strained to open at the lock
Of two millennia. I watched it's heart pulsate,
Mouth like a sea shell move to speak,
"We are the first of Ulster, we warriors
And holy ones. We are the first of all
To raise in gold songs of wars and lovers.
Who stepped a god's print, taking the gods' trail,
And burn, burn and fire, fire,- dig no ring
To reach us, but wait for us, wait for us,
In voices heard before the listening,
In faces that vanish under focus,
Wait for us, wait for us, our scent, our smell
In cracked boortree, water at the dawn well."

8. Castleshane

It's nearly night. The woods of Castleshane
Tighten around Broggan and the Broggan
Hills stretched away to the drain of the dusk
Are settled in their wait. The lunar mask
Will soon descend, the moon's night gown soon fall
After the chord of day is stretched and cut
And the shreds of umbilical spiral
To the dark. When the chapel wall is lit
With first light I will go and enter there
And move bareheaded along the side aisle
And the night's cold still alive in the bone,
Will take to the knee at the altar rail
And bow, and bow that a great grief colour
To west and die in the white of the dawn.

9. Mercator

My map of the world hangs in Mercator,
Stretched Siberia, vast Anctartica,
Contracted land along the equator
At South America and Africa.
Slow light in winter hardened the contour
All along the edges of the ocean,
Rising, fading, rising into my stare
In the image of a crucified man.
Those swollen polar extremities stretched
In the open meridian drew out
At the hollow more and more as I watched
Land and ocean exchange the fading light.
But dark always came before I might see
All retract to its globularity.

10. Wings

The gravity of age is draining out
Thinking ways that once rendered full delight
In younger times, thought then arousing thought
Before those lovers parted with their lot.
Less wise now, being a wiser man, I plant
No flag on any hill and am content
To journey with the swan. An old one now
Moving as the starling, an old one now
Full of migration and autumn moorings,
Full of the rook and gull, full of the eel,
Of things rising to go and falling things,
Full of turn and spin, long cry, long long call.
The gravity of age has drained me dry,
Awaiting wings to land with, wings to fly.

A Wedding Poem

*Written for wedding of Colette Mullen and
Ian Cleary at Mountnugent, Cavan,
November 2nd 2001*

I map the roads where lovers meet.
I mark the straight and the bending way.
I the Lord of earth and heaven
Claim the hour and claim the day.

You ask what piper piped his reel
Or fiddler played the air
To call across the land and sea
Searching out the lover's ear,

And when she heard the tune and turned
And scanned the hills and skies,
Followed where the music came,
And star and day were in her eyes,

And you will ask and ask again
Was it dusk or was it dawn
When they saw each other from afar
And speeded up their step and ran,

But I, I knew them both before
This world was ever made,
Before the pipe or the fiddle came,
Before the hill or sky or glade,

And they have known each other
From a land beyond this lore,
And when they met in mortal form
Knew they'd met somewhere before,

And the place of this first meeting
Is where I forever live,
This is the land without a name,
This is the land of love.

And I will state these final thoughts
I the Lord who hold you dear,
My blessing on this bride and groom
And on all assembled here.

And my blessing on all lovers
That age nor years can sever,
For in the land where I abide
Love is young forever.

Master and Slave

I

Points of fire face our hiding.
Points of fire annoy our guard.
We shift our feet, we shift our stare
Watching the eyes break, eyes
Steady as early stars
Consummate their gathering,
And the beast breaks camouflage.
Dread is our word and dread again
That turns limbs to stone
And our hearts loose in the frame
At the pump of muscle
In the movement of the paw,
We, waiting, waiting, the slow air,
The march, the jig and the reel
Into the frenzy of the kill.

Our ancestors gave much.
Generation after generation
Could not breed the springing hoof
Or poison that might repel,
Generation on generation
Knew no inheritance
But the apparition of the beast,
And flaring eye, and dripping tongue,
The hack around the bone,
The fury of the fang.
Great feeder finishes. The eyes
Recede into the contented pant.
The mane droops and settles.
The long stare and swallow of the spit.

II

Master and slave fall in each other's arm,
Side by side spiral, limb crossed on crossed limb.
Fading eyes fill with moon, their fading warm
Bodies with cooling veins. Though beat of drum,
Though song and call had sounded the alarm
Long before, all danced on, danced down the storm,
And so great feeder draws all to his fate.
Great feeder empty at an empty plate.

They were false prophets who rose in these times
Preaching an age of reason, preaching star
Come in the deep east. They were false whose rhymes
Brandished new worlds, we, who feed on the hour,
Whose hearts, whose heads are born with no new dreams,
Who chew out the last as the first hunger
Still cannot hear in whispering or shout
The point of ripeness is the point of rot.

Past that way where slave face is master's face
In twilight, our tidal surge, the moon glow
Moves its cycle through the soul and there trace
The ancient's writ – our thoughts are the shadow
Of the rage of gods – their verse and chorus
Chanted that, their rhyme, rhythm spoke a flow
Of equal heart, of artery and vein,
The blood of Abel and the blood of Cain.

But more than this. Who would build up Babel,
Who would draw heaven to a destiny
On earth, call revenge of flesh in that call,
And these the earth crush, and none heed their plea,
Nor know the flight from indivisible
God is craving a mother's heart, her eye,
And voices chant that crave, that endless plight.
And voices of day meet the voice of night.

Caesar ate up thirty generations.
From the she- wolf that suckled Romulus
In an Alban hollow passed down the curse
Vein by vein into the imperial veins,
Apex, funnel eye, and gaunt with access
The last Caesar finds no horse for the reins.
Outside, prancing hooves settle. A rider
Dismounts. Light feet move. Loud knock on the door.

And still we watched for Eden. But after
April rain, into May, sighs rise again.
Our eyes lower again. A faint thunder
In the forgotten south stirs distant rain.
Things waver. Our oak, our beech, our alder
Thinly green and now a rattle of chain
Sounds, the crack of a whip and master's bid,
Nails hammered again into bone and wood.

Will earth rise up? Will mother earth rise up?
She the mould of all who sought no judgement
But hill might follow valley. Who will sup
With her, the prophets dead, all who were sent
As slaves of dreams implanted in their sleep?
But those who fed spoke their own testament.
They said she was immune, beyond all fate.
They said her body was immaculate.

Away at the dinosaur's final stand
Where the great spined mover once flared its rule
Remains were found at a lone footprint's end.
They raised it bone by bone from bone dry soil
Spreading their excavations on the sand,
And gave it plastic sockets, joints of steel
Along the vertebrae and nine inch bite.
Then set it up number one exhibit.

(The Secret Verse)

Earth will rise up and strike down her children.
Earth will turn upon them all, her first born brood
And last born of all these, will strike them down,
Mother earth, and bow her anointed head,
And beg no curse, neither beg salvation,
Mother Earth. Barren. Barren. All blood bled.
And Eden's garden empties once again.
And rhymes arise speaking of redemption.

THIRTY-TWO MEDITATIONS

i
I heard from Sigmund Freud
That nineteen centuries after he died,
Christ, in his risen body
Would still avoid
The spot where he was crucified.

But I heard from Carl Jung
That every year around the spring
Christ and the two thieves meet,
Bleeding hands, bleeding feet,
And break into song.

ii
Somewhere when monks
opened the lapis dial
to dip a quill

the lark sprung
from her dewy bed
into the dawn void.

iii
Drink maddened, the sheets
Torn and torn dress
As he vent his rage
On her unwillingness.

Years after and the offspring
Growing, I watch, I see
Its timid smile,
The frightened look in its eye.

iv
POMPEII
Voices entered the ashfall
mould, a hardened shell
of two thousand years

Until the random strike
of an excavator's pick
released their final roars.

v
I met her by a sunset.
As far west as I could go
I walked with her before
the darkness fell to its place.

We stood there together
and spoke of a tomorrow
when we might meet again,
and our steps retrace,

But then, I thought
we'd move on, hand in hand
into the narrow dusk
until the morning's grace

Might discover us,
and leave its first shadow
on the night's imagination
of her forgotten face.

vi
As Donard's head
crowned out
in the breaking ice

a knife of ocean
cut off Ireland
at the joint of Howth.

vii
Death
is never

an experience
of the dier,

but a calculation
of the watcher.

viii

THE PARTING

I thought before hands held
He sang her a final song,
A song she maybe heard of old
At some fair or christening,
And verse after long verse,
A song without a chorus.
It would be maybe evening
When the last note was done,
And when she turned her face
To him, he would be gone.

I thought she followed hill and star
And the song full in her head
Into a springtime later
We stood at the parting bed,
Watching death in love with her,
Her white face, her whiter hair,
And thought a tune began to seep,
Watching the eye's far spill,
Watched the eyelids flicker and fall
As they fell on her first sleep.

ix
On returning from the sea and land
in tattered clothes, bare feet,
at the end of my travels found

the deepest thoughts that greet
do not come at thought's command,
but after thought's defeat.

x
SONATA
After the tonic had sounded
The fledgling spread its wings, soared
Away from the roost
On key after key, chord on chord

Into a later season reappeared
Out of the cloudy south, and landed,
Full wing, body and head
Unto the deserted nest.

xi
What trembling hand
Shaped that mould,
What fire
Brought on the melt,
Pouring wrath
Onto rage,
Pouring Calvin
Into Celt?

xii

I roared out your name
With the lungs' full savagery,
A long unechoed roar
Into the blur of May.
All stopped.
None turned a head
Animal or singing bird,
As still as struck with frost,
Until one upon another
Murmurings and motion came,
And as sound refilled the day
I apologised for the disturbance,
And turned, and moved away.

xiii
Sunset sky
in many.

The dawn
is one.

xiv
Concorde's shadow
Like a Manta Ray
Speeding the ocean floor,

And a sonic boom.
I thought of initiation rites.
And vows of silence.

xv

I knew, the feeble old mother said,
I knew I'd see you again,
Forty years since we parted
And wondered where you'd gone.
But I knew before this day was out
In the world here or the other,
Knew we'd meet before tonight,
Said the old and feeble mother.

xvi

Unless the seeker
is in a melt
and longs to set
they can not
enter the mould
of the C sharp minor
string quartet.

xvii

DANCE OF VOWELS
April. Bud ready.
Sweet shower. Proud sun.
Then forgotten January
Rising from its roost
Spread a whitening wing
Into winds of west,
And curved beak, and spiral claw,
And frost twisted petal mouth,
And frost peeled broom tongue,
The frost sharpened thorn tooth
Drip poison in the thaw.

xviii

And then the sore no longer bled.
For weeks, months I lay and stood
To sew and stitch that gaping hurt.

But an old lament reopened it.
A wound healed in the head
Had broken out in the heart.

xix

CARUSO HIGH C
An archangel's strike
On the gong
of the world.

xx

I though at the post mortem
Rings as trunk growth were found
And one thicker line discovered

Told the state pathologist
That must have been the year
Her beloved parted.

xxi

All pain
divides.

All suffering
unites.

xxii

THE SMILE

As we bade our last farewell
To her, candle above the coffin
And the pale of wax drops

Hardening, felt a tear
Might dampen there, and then
I though a smile began,

A slow smile appear
At the dim light's tremble
On her solemn lips.

xxiii

I hear from thronged Clavary
The dud thump of hammering.
I hear the roars of Christ
To nails piled through the wrist,
Hour after and hour a gale
Of wild noises, wild howl,
He and the hammered thieves.
But the hourglass did not flow,
Their sun refused to budge
Since masks broke on loved faces
And dice throwing soldiers froze.
It's time to hurry away
And free them from their tortures.
It's time to let the sun drop
Into the evening, onto dusk

And the crack as an ash branch
Of bones splintering
Their voices enter silence.
I hear a great shout go up.
Torches are breaking into light
To the sound of brass and drum
Rising around Golgotha.
I see Christ carried shoulder high
Triumphant to the tomb.

xxiv
BURNS
What a brain
Mapped that heart.

What a heart
Fed that brain.

xxv
I thought Beethoven's Ninth
Had crashed and in the gloom
Of dawn crochets and minims found

Strewn all along the ground,
And workers sifting through the length
Of Tochter aus Elysium.

xxvi

The darkest night
Most brightens morning glow.
The brightest light
Throws the darkest shadow.

 xxvii

Oh great sun, rising with blinding glare,
When old age swells your girth
And you droop to a lightless glow,

The dying embers there
Will have wrought immortal shades on earth
When you last sink below.

xxviii

A new light in the sky
Appears in the evening east,
The soul of a dead star

Ten million years after
Its bloated body
Had given up the ghost.

xxix

 I watch a blind man's fingers move
Around the contours of his lover's face,
The fingers of a man born blind
From cheek to chin in stroke and trace,

And touch the forehead with the palms
On eyelids open, eyelids tight,
And knew as I watched his empty eyes
He saw her face in broad daylight.

xxx

Ireland
still steps the jig
That Strongbow danced
To Ferrycarrig.

Israel
still plays upon
The harps that hang
by the Babylon.

xxxi

Midnight and Lough Neagh.
The ghost of the Bann
Meets the ghost
Of the Blackwater.

xxxii

It must be love again.
I hear sounds of the Universe,
I must be falling,
Hearing sounds rising
From galaxy and nebula,
The dying noise in the west
As she rumbles under the world,
And the noisy plough and pole at night.
I hear the hum of the Milky Way
And the distant thunder of Andromeda,
I hear the purr of Sirius
And the crack of an exploding star
Somewhere beyond Orion,
But silent from the east,
Silent on the horizon
In the rise and fall of twilight din
The moon, the moon, the silent moon.
The moon brightening in silence.

The Mist is on
Slieve Gullion

The mist is on Slieve Gullion,
Morning mist at the dark and dawn
Rising under morning star.
The winds of the polar air,
The north sky's limpid breath
Is sudden milk, is sudden cloth
When the first stretch of day
Touches her cold, cold body.

The mist is on Slieve Gullion,
Mist returning in the evening
When the cleared head clouds again
To the south west song.
And the song come spilling tale
Of wild deed and sober deed,
Whisperings, and horn call,
And bearings for the dead.

No mortal eye can witness
A bodily resurrection.
No mortal touch unrap a face
At the rising, forming stone,
But watch from our early Ring
In woollen weave and weave of silk,
The mountain mouths of morning
Feeding on the dawn milk.

Land of my Fathers

(A Meditation for Wales)

I entered down a telescope
Into the bound of galaxy,
Millions motionless in spiral,
Chasm of shade, unmoving flare,
Millions over the clearest night
So vast, so silent there.
But though I heard a faint hum
That the silence seemed to brew,
I thought I heard singing come
From the distant deep of stars
Fading, rising, filling up
Into surging choir sounding
"Land of my Fathers",
And then the vast crescendo
In that fantastic glow
Tapered suddenly away until
The ear could find no more,
Faintest tremble, murmur gone.
I waited maybe half an hour.
It never made return.

I Know The East and Western Thought

I know the east and western thought,
I know that, I know all that,
All the brooding, dreaming men,
Every measurer and prophet,
Drank down their deepest draught,
Drank it year after year
To wake again, I woke again
As dry as dust, dank as glar
For I was wild and I was wild
And the wild turn was in me,
Nor rhyme nor reel,
Nor drum nor drone,
The wild turn, the wild turn,
Nothing fill
And nothing hold
And the wild turn was in me.

I said to all who spoke of art
I know that, I know all that,
Or spoke of some discovery,
Someone's book or someone's name
I turned to them and said the same
All those who called to me,
And morning noon and night thought
The head had clotted up the heart

For I was wild and I was wild
And the wild turn was in me,
Nor rhyme nor reel
Nor drum nor drone
The wild turn, the wild turn,
Nothing fill
And nothing hold
And the wild turn was in me.

I should have went where ancients sat,
I know that, I know all that,
To watch with salmon, watch with swan
Along their flowing moonlit place,
And the tide of night begin to turn
And drain away the lunar skies,
Watch them vague and motionless
And night nor day are in their eyes,
And I was wild and I was wild
And the wild turn was in me,
Nor rhyme nor reel
Nor drum nor drone,
The wild turn, the wild turn,
Nothing fill
And nothing hold
And the wild turn was in me.

The Blind Harper's Prayer

And blest be the nightfall,
And blest be the dawn.
And blest be the dusk again
That calls the evening down.
And blest be its calling
On hollow and on height,
And blest be the bless´ed dark,
And blest be the light.

I pray the lonely moon
As she wakens in the east
To cast her eyefull gently down
On every sleeping beast,
And every beast that stands awake
To follow shadow's flight.
And blest be the bless´ed dark,
And blessed be the light.

I pray the solar lover
To find the moon's pale lips
And both clasp in embrace
Into full eclipse.
And let the full corona there
Dance around its night,
And blest be the bless´ed dark.
And blest be the light.

And Drum Beat Must
Sound Again

Let there be rhythm and rhyme.
Let cataract and waterfall
From clouded mountain
Cascade the ancient theme.
Let drones that made call
Before melody began
Vibrate again, and beat of drum
Come, far off rhythm come,

And drum beat must sound again.
And the great call be heard again.
And old things be made again
In the midwinter dawn.

I rate Burns and Yeats as they
Who most chiselled, cut away
All that clogged and clotted
The early dance and chant,
That old blood run again, sap speed
From the root again, and great
Flow race and race its torrent
Into the thirsting heart,

And drum beat must sound again,
And the great call be heard again,
And old things be made again
In the midwinter dawn.

And let all barnacle and skin
Be shed. All the complication,
This unresolved simplicity
Un cling, un clag, fall free,
And stripped of flower and foilage
All enter the winter again,
Bare branch and bare hedge,
Bare brain on bare bone.

And drum beat must sound again,
And the great call be heard again,
And old things be made again
In the midwinter dawn.

Then singer leave your song aside
And fiddler lay down the bow,
And piper loose the chanter reed
And dancer slow down the dance.
Silence is waiting. Her slow flow
Rising, the fog from cold ground,
Silence. The silence of the silence
Before the first sound.

And drum beat must sound again,
And the great call be heard again,
And old things be made again
In the midwinter dawn.